Champagne

A story that can only begin with him: Dom Pierre Perignon.

If one day in 1668 the prior of the abbey of Hautevillers had not appointed a monk, hitherto unknown, named Pierre Perignon, a man of great culture dedicated to the study of enology, the epic of Champagne would never have taken place. The fate of this wine would certainly have been different.

Dom Prignon served as administrator until he died in 1713.

The vineyards of the abbey, very extensive, became his little kingdom and it was his perfect knowledge and his palate sensitive to let him know all the differences the merits of the various grapes grown, causing the miracle

Contrary to what is thought, it was not this Benedictine who put the bubbles in the wine (process already widely known), but surely it was he who created the assembly of the various grapes of different vineyards, by inventing the Cuvée, a technique that three centuries later is still legally protected.

He managed to improve the quality of the wine, making it fizzy in a permanent way, managing to definitively retain the carbon dioxide released by fermentation.

The sale of this type of wine became increasingly greater and the appreciation of the beverage, as well as in France also arrived in neighboring England; it also had an affordable price compared to other wines, In fact, the Church was exempt from paying certain taxes on the harvest and transport, paid instead by any other secular producer.

The great success of this wine is given by the numerous, sometimes ridiculous attempts of imitation at world level. In every continent is produced a wine "made like Champagne", unfortunately in all other parts of the planet do not grow the same grapes, there is not the same soil and not even the same climate; sometimes the method is also lacking.

Success was and still is planetary.

Champagne means Victory (but you console yourself even after a defeat), it means Celebration, Greetings, Romance and unforgettable moments, as well as exceptional taste.

I am not a Sommelier, nor a fine connoisseur, just an enthusiast, a person who occasionally drinks the best drink on Earth (and would like to do so more often). It is said that even the less renowned Champagne is better than any other type of wine and I fully agree: for the product, for the history, for the processing and the laws that regulate the production and finally the Grandeur.

I am an admirer of this wonder of nature, perfected later by the human being, I am a lover of its historicity, its geo-location and its grandeur worldwide.

With the help of bibliographic searches and in "net" I would like to transmit to you the information of which now I have. This is a booklet for newbies or total unwittings, like me. It will serve to excite some of you at Champagne and over time could lead you to the most detailed knowledge of the product, even buying some bottles to begin to understand it better.

The first time I drank Champagne I was in Cortina d'Ampezzo, I was 18 years old and I liked skiing, even now skiing is the only real sport I practiced, when I can go, in recent years I did not, unfortunately.

At what time I lived in Ferrara and with friends, often on weekends, we went to visit another, hairdresser, employed throughout the winter season, at a well-known coiffeur in Cortina. Obviously our economic possibilities were scarce and we could not afford to stay in the town, where at the time you paid for the air you breathed. Nearby there were many villages that were our case: San Vito, Tai or Borca di Cadore. During the day we shared between the slopes of Faloria and Cristallo, there were those who went to Socrepes. In the evening we went to the Disco of the Hotel Europa which, if I remember correctly at that time was called Biblò.

During the evening, there was always some young or old-timers, in the mood for megalomanias and exhibitionism, so that Champagne Magnum's laps left for all those present in the restaurant, obviously all offered.

At that time I didn't realize how delicious it was, the Champagne was sipped to act, the time was dedicated to all the magnificent girls in the room, and when I could talk to a girl, I wasn't arguing about wines.

At that age you think you really are on top of the world, but unfortunately the following year I began to work and I came back down to earth.

In my life I have only done two professions, the current one as a civil servant , interspersed with some years of Computer and Artistic Representations, in the 2000s.

However, since then, I continued to attend Cortina even as an adult, for family reasons.

When I was 22, with my girlfriend of the time, we went to Paris; we rented a car and we went to the Champagne region. Not even then was I interested in wines, except superficially.

I was still missing a real and immersive Tour of the Champagne Route, what the so-called experts of "bubbles" do.

Many years later, invited to a lunch in a beautiful country house in the province of Bologna, where the banquet was held, I saw leaning on a wall of the entrance loggia, two whole cases of "Veuve Cliquot" with the 24 bottles that were showing off them, with the beautiful orange label.

Some time later, I started buying some bottles of champagne, of course when I could afford it, trying to change the brand of each purchase.

At that time I lived alone, even though I was engaged.

I began to taste "bubbles" with light meals but also with typical Emilian cuisine and anything was pefetta with a bottle of Champage.

At the age of 50 it became a real passion, sometimes a topic of discussion, when I find suitable interlocutors, very rarely.

Index

Title: Champagne

In France, the Law of July 1927, which extended a pre-existing one, with its successive modifications, the last important in 2001, defines in detail the collection, vinification and sale of the product:

Areas and vines are well defined

The grapes must be exclusively of three types (there were another 5 but now they have fallen, although some Maisons still use them)

Harvesting and vinification follow a precise, ancient and peremptory process.

Terroir

The hectares of land, currently occupied by vines are about 35 thousand, with a denomination of controlled origin (AOC).

They are distributed in 4 main areas: the Massif de Reims, the Marne Valley, the Còte de Blancs and the Aube and Aisne area.

We are describing a region in the northeast of France at about 150 kilometers from Paris, bordering Belgium: the Champagne-Ardennes.

No producer or winemaking company, can call their wine "Chamapgne" outside these areas, the French Government Law is peremptory on this.

Geologically the soil is chalky, calcium cabonate, called "craie", and up to 70 million years ago covered with sea water.

In more recent times, and we are talking about 10 million years, after the retreat of the sea, violent and frequent movements of the earth's crust, broke and modified the ground again making it resurface in the part that had remained immersed, which has been impregnated with minerals, sea salts and organic compounds.

Above the chalky level, about 200 meters high, there is the fertile soil, which resting on the cretaceous layer, absorbs all the peculiarities and characteristics, unique and essential to the vine plants.

The uniqueness of this area derives from this chalky crust on which it rests.

Its functions are to store heat and return it to the soil when needed, ensure a perfect drainage of excess water and absorb large amounts of moisture that will then be returned to the soil in the summer seasons particularly dry.

Vines find in this environment, minerals and organic characteristics that converge in the berries of its grapes giving these wines a unique personality in nature.

The region is very often affected by the icy winds that come from the Atlantic Ocean after crossing Normandy.

This hostile climate is slightly mitigated by the forests present on the hills of the area: the tall trees present in the area also have the function of reducing the percentage of humidity present in the air, by harmoniously promoting the production of grape bunches.

In the winter and up to late spring, wandering around the region you can see small heaters, inserted between the rows, fully automated and managed by a computer center, which heat the plants, preserving the gems of the vines from the terrible frosts that could occur.

Also for the storms and hailstorms the "vignerons" have foreseen the adequate measures with covers of the vines, too precious for them.

In the region, the Municipal or Locality areas are 324 and are classified in "Cru" being defined according to the value of their grapes: Cru, Premier

Cru and Grand Cru, a value that is based on the quality of the grapes produced in these areas.

The municipalities that can boast the title of "Grand Cru" are only 17 of the 324 mentioned above.

Only the owners of the "Maison" who have all their vineyards in these places can boast in the label of their product the words Grand Cru.

The massif of Reims

The woods cover this plateau between Rheims and Epernay. To the north near the valleys of Ardre and Vesle, the height drops as well as to the south, approaching the river Marne.

Pinot Noir develops its enormous qualities on this chalky massif.

In the vicinity of Bouzy, south of the massif, these grapes make a structured and strong product while to the east the vines of Verzenay give an aromatic wine.

In Mailly, a village located on the north side, the Pinot Noir produces an elegant and round wine.

Seeing many vineyards exposed to the north can surprise the visitor, but it is the place where the grapes mature in the evening. At sunset, light winds push the warm air (which has formed in high ground on sunny days) between the plants at low altitude.

In these places is also noted the rare presence of Chardonnay vines, but only in the eastern part, the one sheltered from the icy winds of the west, in the municipalities of Trepail and Villers Marmery.

The aromas of Pinot Noir are those of berries, blackberries, currants and raspberries.

With the term "Blancs de Noir" are determined the white wines produced escusivamente from black berried grapes, Pinot Noir and Pinot Meunier; the pulp inside the berries is however white and the skins are not macerated.

La Grande Vallée de la Marne

This area is located on the slope created by the reliefs and the river.

On the two banks, and also on the slopes and near the tributary streams of the Marne, the grapes grow.

The part located closer to Epernay is called La Grande Vallée de la Marne, in this area is still high production of Pinot Noir with a higher production of 60 percent of crops.

Going west instead, the cultivations of Pinot Meunier increase, more rustic and traditional vine, suitable for even more hostile climates.

La Côte des Blancs

To the south of Epernay, the Côte des Blancs cliff stretches for a length of about 15 kilometres; the hilly areas are oriented towards the east and here the vines are well sheltered from the icy gusts of winds coming from the west.

Here the Chardonnay grape is predominant and the wine becomes

Blanc de Blancs, that is, it is produced only with white grapes.

Chardonnay has very delicate grapes, give fresh and elegant notes, it is a very sensitive vine for which it is well cared for and sheltered from the frequent icy days of spring; it is the grape preferred by the great Maison for their cuveè. To the south is the "Clos de Mesnil" grape variety owned by Krug.

La Côte de l'Aube

From Bar sur Aube to Bar sur Seine, of outlines this coast.

Here the subsoil is not particularly chalky, remaining however calcareous has inside many marble intrusions, as in the nearby region of Burgundy.

It is the homeland of Rosè, here both Pinot Noir and Chardonnay were cultivated and the fact that the land is different from other areas of Champagne, makes the delicate work of the Chef de Cave employed in the many wineries. These professionals find and assemble wines of different origins in order to produce fine Champagne.

The Vines

As described before, in order to be produced Champagne wines must have an exclusive use of three noble wines indicated by law:

- Pinot Noir, from fine black grapes and infuse vigorous and strong aromas

- **Pinot Meunier, from more rustic black grapes, to give longevity and**

endurance to the wine

- **Chardonnay, from white grapes, full of lightness, elegance and freshness**

The cultivation of these vines is really meticulous, to have the first fruits you have to wait at least four years from the installation of the plant, while the lifespan of the same plant is about thirty years.

Usually the small seedling of vines, is grafted in spring and takes root in warm greenhouses of small towns in the region.

Throughout the area, the vines are planted in an extremely orderly and rational manner; as you walk along the plants, you will notice the metallic inlays to which the vines are bound.

The entire cycle of vine culture begins after the harvest, in late autumn.

The soil is enriched using black sands and ashes that arrive from the surrounding quarries; this compound accumulates near the vineyard and is then spread along the edges of the rows, joining them to appropriate fertilizers.

When spring is approaching, pruning operations begin, using one of the three methods allowed by the Law.

- Cordon Royat

- Chablis

- Guyot

The vine stumps, after thirty years of life are replaced with other younger ones, at the end of these operations the soil is plowed.

In May the vine blooms, and according to the tradition and experiences of local farmers, the harvest will come after a hundred days from flowering;

before the harvest will be carried out a further pruning, removing the large leaves that prevent the sun rays from penetrating and give the right ripening to the plain.

The Harvest

The "vignerons" wait with great trepidation on the day of the harvest; at the end of the hard and hard work, it represents the concrete result of their winter processing, to which they have dedicated time and effort.

Usually the beginning of the harvest takes place on the third week of September, in that period the Village Festivals multiply and you can breathe a joyful and sparkling.

The grapes are harvested by hand; thousands of volunteers, students and specialized technicians come from all over France and the world.

At dawn the harvest begins, but under the possible scorching sun or heavy rain the harvest is immediately stopped, to avoid the spontaneous fermentation of the grapes.

The "mannequins", wicker or plastic baskets, are used to lay the bunches of grapes.

For the transport of the baskets full of bunches, small wagons are used with very soft and balanced shock absorbers, so as not to dent or dodge the grapes during transport at the Maison.

The grapes will arrive in perfect condition and the berries not perfectly ripe, with defects or crushed will be eliminated with the operation called "epluchage".

The latter is a part of the activity that allows a rigorous selection of grapes, in order to avoid later bad fermentation or unpleasant flavors of wine and make sure to obtain an excellent effervescence.

During the operations, it is necessary to be very careful for Pinot Noir and Pinot Meunier as the dark skin tends to color the must of the pressing and this should not happen, in order not to depreciate the visual quality of the wine. At the press the grapes must come in excellent condition so as not to affect the characteristics of the final product.

Obviously, such a careful harvest of the grapes is carried out by hand and by French law it is very forbidden to harvest them mechanically.

The Pressing

Centuries of work experience have spread rules and instruments in the production of Champagne, in all its stages of processing.

The presses called "pressoirs" make very delicate squeezing, slowly and constantly, even modern pneumatic ones.

After loading the press with grapes of the same "cru", that is from the same production area, the slow pressing begins.

The press is designed and built in such a way as to press on the grapes in a constant and soft way as it must absolutely avoid the crushing of the skins and prevent the must from coloring.

After a first filtering, the wine falls into the vat called "belon".

The quantity of grapes that can be contained in the "champenoise" press is four thousand kilograms and this quantity is called "marc".

From this quantity the "vignerons" can then extract a maximum of 2665 liters of must.

With the first 2050 liters you get the "cuvee" then with another 410 liters you get the "premiere taille". while from the last 205 liters the "deuxiemme taille" is obtained.

Only the must produced with the "cuvee" is used for the great Champagne, the "taille" have more bitter and intense flavors.

The must is then decanted in large vats and clarified (or we try to eliminate all particles and foreign bodies), in a natural or artificial way, this operation is called "debourbage".

Clarification takes place by centrifuge or precipitation, adding bentonite; the majority of producers still use the ancient method of cooling the must, gradually bringing it to a temperature just below the degree of freezing.

At the end of the "debourbage" the must obtained is ready for the barrels in the cellars.

The First Alcoholic Fermentation

The fermentation process takes place in "barriques", oak barrels with a capacity of 205 liters, or as modern producers use in vitrified steel barrels.

The temperature, during the process, must be constantly of 18 degrees, then the yeasts are added from selected cultures and here occurs the transformation of the sugar molecules contained in the must, in molecules of ethyl alcohol and carbon dioxide.

At the end of this process, a few months later, the carbon dioxide was released into the air as the casks are not watertight and the still white wine had an acidity much lower than the previous must.

Toward the end of winter, as the temperature rises, the wine continues to ferment and here we will have another process: malolactic.

The malic acid contained in the product degrades to lactic acid and again to carbon dioxide; the longer this process lasts, the more the champagne will have caseine notes.

At the end of the malolactic process (some producers do not) it is necessary to deposit again the tartar corpuscles loose in the liquid, but it will be enough to aerate the cellar and lower the temperature to start the procedure.

The Assemblage

In spring comes a time dedicated to an important operation: the preparation of the "cuvees", that is, the preparation of what the final consumer will benefit.

They use the base wines of the current vintage that are mixed with reserve wines stored in the cellar, after a rigorous and careful tasting.

The "cuvee" is the business card of the winemaker, his work done with dedication and effort; the taste characterizes the Maison and the Chef de Cave, that is, the cellar manager skilfully blends new wine and different areas in order to re-create every year the traditional taste of the Maison.

If you want to create a "millèsimè", you will use wines from different areas but of the same vintage, differently for the "sans anneè" we could have wines from different years but from the same areas.

If you want to get a "rosè" you must do this at the time of "tirage" (see next paragraph) by adding a small percentage of red wine that will color the must, depending on the choices of the company from a fine red to a light red.

Some companies also use 100 different wines for their blending.

Second fermentation: the Tirage

After processing the "cuveè" in large vats, the product will be bottled, adding about 24 gr. sugars and yeasts per liter.

In this way the wine will undergo a second fermentation in the bottle and you will get the pressure of about 6 Atmospheres inside it.

The bottles will then be deposited on the "lattes", wooden shelves, ordered along the ancient cellars made from chalk quarries.

In this process the temperature must not exceed 10-11 degrees centigrade; the bottles remain on the lattes minimum 12 months for Champagne "sans anneè" while for "millesimè"
the months become minimum 36.

Producers have a tendency to create reserves of prestigious and memorable Champagne wines, known as "Grand Cuveè". The wine verne left lying on the "lattes" to ferment on the lees 5, 6 or 10 years.

Exceptional wines are made; the "degorgement" (following paragraphs) is made at the last moment, just before the sale.

The alcoholic fermentation is repeated, but this time the carbon dioxide remains trapped in the bottle and it will be mixed to the wine giving life to the "pris de mousse", making the wine sparkling once uncorked.

The Remouage

At the end of the second alcoholic fermentation, inside the bottle are formed deposits of lees called "lie", the cellar workers must absolutely eliminate them.

The bottles are then taken from the "lattes" and placed with the neck down, on wooden easels, hinged at the top and placed in the shape of an inverted V, in which holes have been drilled, these easels are called "pupitres".

The remouage consists in turning the bottles about a quarter of a turn each day, in order to move and drop down the scum deposited during aging.

The "pupitre" was specially built to be able to progressively tilt the bottles from 45 to 90 degrees, with the passage of days.

The operators or "remouers" in a period of time of eight weeks, will shake, turn and incline the bottles up to bring them in a vertical upside down position, so as to force all the storage accumulated on the inner sides of the bottle to fall against the crown cap, leaving clear all the rest of the wine.

Most of the Maison has now replaced the "remouers" with modern machines called "gyropalettes", only the Grand Maison, very well funded and economically structured, prefer the old system.

At the end of the "remouage" the bottles are placed neck down "sur pointe" waiting for the next phase of "degorgement".

The Degorgement

To eliminate all the residues of lees, which over time have been deposited in the neck of the bottle near the crown cork, it is necessary to proceed to a further and very important activity of eleboration of the wine.

Only the neck of the bottle, is immersed for a few centimeters in a liquid solution at the temperature of -25 degrees centigrade; the deposit of scum freezes in an instant and is made viscous.

At this point, with a quick gesture of the operator or the machine, the bottle is uncorked and the internal pressure, created by carbon dioxide, allows the ice of lees that has been created inside the bottle to escape quickly.

This operation called "degorgement a la glasse" was invented in 1884 by Armad Walfart.

Once this operation was carried out only by hand by the most experienced employees and took the name of "degorgement a la voleè", swirling the bottle upwards and at the same time it was uncorked.

Uncorking the bottle and letting out the ice block, obviously a small amount of wine is dispersed; then the topping up or the "dosage" made with the "liqueur de expedition", a composite of other Champagne wine and selected cane sugars.

This determines the obtaining of the type of Champagne, from the

"Brut" to the "Demi-Sec".

Immediately after the "expedition", the bottle is closed with a cork called "buchon" which is closed in a metal cage called "muslet".

The quality of cork is fundamental for the final characteristics of Champagne.

The bottles are then shaken to amalgamate the new part with the rest of the liquid, operation called "poignettage", then are returned to the cellar for a short period of stabilization.

The Label

The final phase, before marketing, involves the application of the label, the "dress" of the Maison.

On the complete labels are indicated: the name of the Maison, the name of the Wine Champagne, the name of the Cuveè, the vintage of production in the case of "millesimè", the alcoholic degrees, the style (Brut - extrabrut.ecc.), the area of production of the wine, the capacity of the bottle and often also the date of "degorgement", finally the type of Poducer (see next paragraphs).

Conservation of Champagne

Once purchased, the Champagne should be stored in a cool cellar at 10-12 degrees centigrade, protected from drafts; The bottles must be laid down horribly so that the inside of the cork is always in contact with the liquid and avoid drying by leaking the gas.

Champagne should be drunk immediately after purchase, a long stay in your cellars or in modern refrigerated cabinets, could affect the color and especially the flavor.

Serving temperature

Champagne is served at a temperature of about 6-8 degrees Celsius, so very cool.

The ideal way to serve it is in a bucket filled with water and ice, the bottle should be immersed about 20 minutes before uncorking.

Do not use the refrigerator or freezer.

The Bottle

The gifts of Champagne bottles are extremely strange and have the following names:

Quart	18,75 or 20 cl equal to one flute
Demie	37,5 cl equal two flute
Bouteille	75 cl equal 6-8 flutes
Magnum	2 bottle (1.5 litres)
Jeroboam	4 bottle (3 litres)
Rèhoboam	6 bottle (4,5 litres)
Mathusalem	8 bottle (6 litres)
Salmanazar	12 bottle (9 litres)
Balthazar	16 bottle (12 litres)
Nabuchodonosor	20 bottel (15 litres)
Salomon	24 bottle (18 litres)

| Primat | 36 bottle (27 litres) |
| Melchisedec | 40 bottle (30 litres) |

The names of the bottles, as described above, refer to mythical and biblical characters.

The Maison Taittinger, has put on the market a format of 25 liters that called Souverain.

It has been ascertained however, that Champagne gives its best yield in the traditional 75 cl bottle or in Magnum, where the ratio between wine and volume of the bottle is optimal for the success of the wine.

Flutè or Cup of Champagne

Now that the Champagne is ready and bottled and just waiting to be served, there is a problem: which glass is used for drinking?

The generic white wine is usually served in tulip shaped glasses, the red wine in a large glass with an open cup. How do you serve champagne at the table?

The answer is : Flute. The narrow and elongated shape of this glass enhances and accentuates the flow of bubbles towards the top, while the small surface accentuates the aromas.

Glossary

AOC: Appellation d'Origine Controllèe. French denomination equivalent to the Italian DOC. It is used for wines of superior quality whose production is regulated by law. AOC wines fall into the category of the European Community "VQPRD" Quality Wines from a specific Region .

Assemblage: Wine cutting , that is an operation that consists in mixing wines with different and determined characteristics in order to create the Cuvée.

Barrique: Small barrel of fine oak wood. In the Champage region, the traditional barrique is called "pièce" and contains 225 liters of wine. Some producers still use, for the best Champage, oak barrels for the first alcoholic fermentation or for the aging of the wines used in the following assembly.

Batonnage: Action that puts in suspension the scum that was previously created and deposited on the bottom. This operation takes place after the first alcoholic fermentation and promotes the autolysis of yeasts. It aims to increase the body of the wine and the better development of some aromas.

Bidule: Plastic capsule placed inside the crown cap "bouchon courone" before the "pris de mousse". Its shape promotes the collection of sediments and keeps the ice bulge compact during the "degorgement".

Blanc de Blancs: Champagne wines produced exclusively with white Chardonnay grapes.

Blanc de Noirs: Champagne wines produced exclusively with Pinot Noirs or Pinot Meunier grapes.

Bouquet: Set of olfactory and retro-olfactory scents:
primary: sensations derived from grapes

secondary: sensations derived from fermentation and ageing

tertiary sector: complex aromas deriving from aging

Cave: Cellar. The limestone soil of the Champagne region, allowed to dig deep without using supporting structures. Very long and huge tunnels where the temperature is constant at 10-12 degrees centigrade and the humidity of the air at 70%. It is estimated that there are at least 250 kilometers of tunnels throughout the region and some of them reach the length of 40 meters in depth.

Cèpage: Grape variety. Champagne wines are produced with three varieties: Chardonnay, Pinot Noir and Pinot Meunier. Black grapes reach 2/3 of the total. The entire production is regulated by the Champagne Statut.

Chardonnay: White grape whose grapes bring finesse and elegance to the wines.

Clos: Vineyard closed. They are vineyards with the highest quality of grapes and with which are produced exceptional Champagne. Usually the name of the vineyard is indicated on the label as in the case of Krug "Clos de Mesnil" or Philoponnat "Clos de Goisses".

Collage: Clarification of wine. Wine making technique that aims to make clear the wine without altering its color and characteristics. This action is carried out by filtration or by the use of organic substances whose ability is to coagulate and precipitate the impure particles that remain in suspension in the liquid.

Coupage: Blending of wines from different vineyards, is done to balance and expand the range of products.

Cru: Vineyard of specific quality and a certain area. In the Champagne region the cru scale has a geographical base and a price index derived from the quality of the grapes and individual vineyards. From top to bottom you have:

Grand Cru

Premier Cru

Cru

Cuvée: You have three different meanings.

- Identifies the must of the first pressing with 4050 kilograms are obtained citca 2050 liters of "cuvèe" and 500 liters of "taille".

- It indicates the blending of wines from different vineyards, cru and vintages.

– The Maison use this name to identify their best and most prestigious Champagnes such as: Laurent Perrier Grand Siècle or Perrier -Jouet Belle Epoque.

Debourbage: Decantation. Operation carried out on the must before the main fermentation to remove the coarser impurities present after crushing. It happens by simple gravity, leaving the must for 10-12 hours in order to deposit on the bottom residues of skins or pips.

Degorgement: Disgorgement carried out after the "remouage" to eliminate the sediments of lees that were formed during the aging of the wine. The bottles are immersed in a neck facing down in a cooling solution at -25 degrees centigrade, for a few centimeters. The resulting ice block, compacted by the "bidule" is expelled by removing the crown cap temporarily placed. The small amount of wine that comes out is enriched with the "liqueur d'expetition" and the bottle is finally capped with multilayer cork.

Dosage: Introduction of the "liqueur d'expedition" which is carried out immediately after the "degorgement". It is a liquid solution composed of sugars of cane and other wine. Sugars are released in a variable percentage according to the type of Champagne desired. The terms **"pas dosè"** or **"nature"** indicate the total absence of sugar. Below are the definitions referring to the percentages of sugar released:

1. Brut Nature : residual sugar not exceeding 3 gr/L
2. Extra Brut: residual sugar not exceeding 6 gr/L
3. Brut: 15 gr/L
4. Extra Dry: 20 gr/L
5. Sec: 35 gr/L
6. Demi Sec: 50 gr/L
7. Doux: more than 50 gr/L

Fermentation: Champagne wines undergo two fermentations. The first alcoholic fermentation takes place in wooden barrels or large vitrified steel vats; the second takes place in the bottle (pris de mousse). To the still wines obtained with the first fermentation (assembled in cuvèe) are added cane sugars and yeasts after bottling (tirage). The bottles are then placed in the cellars, placed in a gloomy position on the "lattes" for many months or even years. Yeasts, in this second process, cause a fermentation by transforming the sugar molecules into alcohol and carbonic andidride. The fineness of the "perlage" and its persistence in the glass depend on the care with which this operation is carried out and also on the duration of aging. At the end of the period, the pressure inside the bottle is about 6/7 atmospheres and the alcohol content is slightly increased.

Gyropalette: Automatic system that allows to mechanically perform the "remouage" of the bottles with perfect results. They need less space than the old "pupitre".

Lattes: Wooden strips of 1 cm. thick where the bottles are placed in the cellars.

Levures: yeasts. Naturally occurring plant cells on the skin of grape berries. They reproduce in the must and cause alcoholic fermentation. They are organisms of different types and are grouped in families. Those selected in the Champagne region characterize the final product.

Liquer de dosage o de expèdition: Mixture of wines and sugars added to the liquid after "degorgement".

Liquer de tirage: Solution of yeasts and sugars added to the wine in bottle fermentation to give rise to the "pris de mousse".

Mèthode Champenoise: Classic method of sparkling by a second alcoholic fermentation in bottle. With the new EU legislation the term has been replaced by "Mèthode traditionelle".

Millèsimè: Particularly good year for the grapes that are harvested for the creation of wines of a single vintage. It is marketed at least three years after harvest. In this case the year is indicated on the label of the bottle.

Monocru: Grapes from a single "Cru".

Mousse: Foamy formation created in the glass when pouring a sparkling wine. This refers to the development of bubbles as a whole. The qualities of Champagne are also evaluated by observing the thickness of the foam on the surface of the product.

Must: The grape juice obtained by pressing the berries; its composition is very complex, there are hundreds of substances but the main ones are: water, sugar and acids. In the Champagne region the must is always white, even if obtained from black grapes, as the coloring substances are present only on the skin of the grape. Thanks to the delicate and soft squeezing the skins are not broken or crushed excessively, so the must is not colored. To create Rosè wines, the process is different.

Perlage: Term little diffused and little used in France. This name indicates the set of bubbles of carbon dioxide that develop in the glass after pouring the product.

Pinot Meunier: Black grape variety, representing almost 40% of all production. It's mostly present in the Marne Valley west of Epernay and in cold wet places. Meunier means miller. The grapes are covered with a white patina reminiscent of flour.

Pinot Noir: Black grape variety. It occupies 1/3 of the viticultural area and is mainly present in the area of Reims. It has a very pleasant bouquet and has persistence and resistance to aging.

Pointe: Tip. Vertical upside down position of a bottle. In this way are kept the bottles that have finished the phase of "remouage" waiting for the "degorgement".

Pressoir: Pressing press. They are traditionally wide and low, in order not to violently crush the grapes and have a capacity of 4000 kg. called "marc". Modern ones have pneumatic pressing, constantly soft and much faster than old presses.

Pressurage: Crushing. It is used to extract the juice from the grapes and to separate the solid residues of other materials such as grape seeds and skins.

Pris de Mousse. Foam. The second fermentation makes the wine foamy due to the intake of carbon dioxide created by the added yeasts. In the

Champagne region it is forbidden to produce wine in other ways.

Pupitres: Special wooden easels formed by two panels hinged to the top and drilled on the sides to insert the bottles during the "remouage" phases.

Rd, Recentement Degorgè. Trademark registered by Maison Bollinger. Diction for high quality wines, usually "millesimè" that have undergone a recent disgorgement. The exact date is indicated on the label.

Remouage: Shaking. Oparation with which the deposits of dregs present on the inner sides of the bottle during the foaming, are gradually dropped towards the cork. Once it was performed by the "remouers" now it is done with the "gyropalette".

Rosé: Champagne Wine of rosé color obtained with "saigneè" method that is leaving the skins of red grapes to macerate a few more hours or at the time of "tirage" is added a small part of red wine reserve. It is always invited to ask the sommelier if the rosé is of assembly or maceration.

Saint Vincent: Patron Saint of winegrowers. He is the patron saint of Burgundy and by extension of all the vineyards of France. Numerous village festivals are celebrated in his honor. The day is January 22.

Sans annèe, Sa: Indicates the most common Champagnes, obtained by the blending of wines from different vineyards, "cru" and vintages. No vintage is indicated on the bottle.

Sigle dei Produttori:

CM: Cooperative de Manipulation. Cooperative to which members bring their grapes and which provides for the processing and sale of wines.

MA: Marche d'acheteur or Marche Auxiliare. When the brand does not belong to the person who processes the Champagne. It is designed for special or commercial needs.

ND: Negociant Distributeur. A shopkeeper who buys, labels and sells elaborate bottles the seller.

NM: Negociant Manipulant. It is a producer who buys grapes, musts and wines but also cultivates his own vineyards and processes in premises owned by him. Many major companies work this way.

R: Winemaker, who has others process but markets under his own brand.

RM: Recoltant Manipulant. Great "Maison" of Champagne, who cultivate their own vineyards, collect, process and sell under their own brand. The most prestigious one.

SR: The company is made up of "vignerons" from the same family, who come together to share their vineyards and process wine. This gives you more possibilities for assembly and sales.

Taille: Pruning. Practice that regulates the cultivation of the vine. For the French Law the three usable methods are: Cordon Royal, Chablis and Guyot.

Terroir: Soil with particular morphological and geographical characteristics. A term that includes more complex aspects including: soil, subsoil, slope and exposure. The roots of the vineyards sink into a particular layer of chalk that can reach in certain areas up to 200 m. thick. It's a soil rich in minerals, thermally stabilized and with constant drainage.

Tirage: is the phase in which yeast and sugar are added to the wine to initiate the procedure of the second fermentation in bottle. This triggers the "pris de mousse".

Tonneau: Wine barrel. In France it has two meanings: it is a synonym of "barrique" 225 liters or in the current language of the employees it can mean 4 "barriques".

Vendage: Harvest time.

Veiellissement sur lies: Aging on lees deposits. After the completion of the fermentation, this phase of aging of Champagne wines takes place. Through the autolysis of yeasts, with very evolved aromas compared to the original must. After this step the aromatic structure of the wine is further enriched.

Vigneron: Grape grower or vineyard owner.

Vignoble: Vineyard, vineyard plot. Indicates the whole area suitable for producing a derminated wine.

Vin de rèserve: Reserve wine. Older wine, from previous years and of high quality. Used in the formation of cuvée to give Champagne not "millesimè" greater complexity and body.

Some aphorisms and quotes about Champagne wine

- *I drink Champagne when I'm happy and when I'm sad. I sometimes drink it when I'm alone. When I have company I consider it mandatory. I sip it when I'm not hungry and I drink it when I have. Otherwise I don't drink it, unless I'm very thirsty.*

  Madame Elisabeth Lauriston (Vedova Bollinger)

- *In diplomacy, where it is fought at the table, the clinking of the flutes replaces the noise of the cannons.*
  Anonymous

- *Champagne, the winner deserves it, the loser needs it.*
  Napoleon Bonaparte

- *Great love stories start with champagne and end with chamomile.*
  Valery Larbaud – Poet

- *Sooner or later there will come a time in every woman's life when the only thing that can help is a bottle of champagne.*
  Bette Davis – actress

- *I have often observed that in the homes of married people Champagne is rarely of good quality*
  Oscar Wilde – writer

- *Penicillin cures people, but champagne makes people happy.*
  Alexander Fleming

Champagne producers

The Champagne producers, famous and not, are several hundred. I chose some to make the story, telling some vicissitudes in reference to the activities of the various types of Champagne produced. It is a brief historical panorama of viticulture.

The following "Maison" are placed in alphabetical order:

AYALA

The starting point of his bottles is the Chateau d'Ay farm in Marenil sur Ay. They are the best Cru of the Mountains of Reims and Cote de Blanc and make this wine.

BOLLINGER

Athanasio Louis Emmanuel de Villermont was the founder of the "Maison". The family lived in the area of Ay, Cruis and Verzenay since 1400. After many vicissitudes the property passes to the Bollinger. Elizabeth de Lauriston, widow of Jacques, takes the reins of the company in 1941. Elizabeth was called "Madame bicyclette" because at all hours of the day and evening, she walked the rows of grapes, giving directions, helping and controlling the work.

Highlights of the "maison" are the Brut "millesime".

CHARLES HEIDSECK

"Maison" founded in 1875, but became important in 1805. They were the first to supply champagne wine in the United States at the time of the Civil War.

Prohibition was the golden age of the company.

Their cellars in Reims date back two thousand years.

GOSSET

Ancient documents indicate the Gossets, lords and politicians in Ay as early as 1531. Purely red vines, private customers and great connoisseurs of Bouzy. The French jet-set was their client: Aznavour, Belmondo, Ingrid Berman, Debrè, Simenon....

KRUG

"Maison", founded in 1843. The family motto is - Produce very little but very well - .

"Private Cuvée" and very rare thousands are known worldwide for finesse and quality.

Krug consumers form an Elite Club, a circle that cannot be very extensive considering the selling prices.

Moet et Chandon

She is the "Maison" leading exporter of Champagne wines. She makes the special "cuvée" Dom Perignon.

MUMM

Everyone knows the label "Cordon Rouge", many forget the company. Famous also the Cremant of Cramant, in the Còte de Blancs.

PERRIER JOUET

In the heart of Cramant, only two names: Cuvèe "Belle Epoque" bottled in a bottle created in 1920 by master glassmaker Emile Gallè; it has Art Nouveau floral decorations. Then the Rosè "millesimè" "Blason de France".

PHILOPPONAT

Owners of the Clos de Goisses, a corner of paradise in the Champagne region. The shadow of this vineyard, projected on the water of the river, reproduces a bottle of champagne. Fabulous "millesimè".

POL ROGER

Twenty-five thousand square meters of cellars, located on three levels in Epernay. Production of Brut and Rosè extraordinary.

ROEDERER

Supplier of the Zar, creator of the renowned Cristal Cuvée in transparent bottle and the less known but much appreciated Cart Blanche.

TAITTINGER

"Maison" relativamente recente rispetto a molte altre , fondata nel 1932. Produce il Comtes de Champagne Blanc de Blacs e buoni Rosè.

VEUVE CLIQUOT PONSARDIN

Nicole Barbe Ponsardin remains widow of Francois Cliquot to 27 years, from this episode the name of the company. 265 hectares of vineyards and many contracts with the small "vignerons".

Luca Ramari

61, former civil servant now retired.

Not a sommelier or even a connoisseur

Only a lover and an admirer of the historicity of champagne wines

Bibliografia

Enrico Guagnini – Lo Champagne – Sansoni Enciclopedie Pratiche – Firenze 1979

Lazaroni, Garuti, Casiraghi – Champagne- Bivino Editore – Brescia 2008

Gerard Liger Belair – Bollicine – Einaudi- Torino 2005

Andrea Gori – Manuale di conversazione sullo Champagne – Trenta Editore – Firenze 2012

With the help of machine translators I translated this little glossary. I apologize for all the mistakes that might be there. However, the substance of the argument remains solid and flawless.
Thank you all so much.

Questa è la seconda edizione, in lingua inglese. La prima edizione in lingua italiana è del 2015.